AF406742

Electric Pressure Cooker

Easy Recipes for Delicious and Healthy Meals

Amanda Hopkins

backing by the trademark owner. All trademarks and brands within this book are for clarifying purposes only and are owned by the owners themselves, not affiliated with this document.

Table of Contents

x

Chapter 1: Introducing Electric Pressure Cooker Benefits

A new trend among people who eat healthy and enjoy cooking with minimal mess and time is the modern pressure cooker. This type of cooking instrument has been around for several decades, but the new models come to the market vastly improved and with health and convenience in mind. When introducing electric pressure cooker benefits, you have to consider that you'll get tasty meals packed with nutrients. There's no need to spend hours in the kitchen, standing over multiple pots and pans.

How an Electric Pressure Cooker Works

If you're not familiar with the mechanics of an electric pressure cooker, they're pretty simple. The food is cooked inside a pot at high heat, and the steam that builds up inside that sealed environment conducts all the cooking. The heat and the pressure rise from the heating source throughout the pot. It's a clean, easy way to prepare food and eat well. Most cookers are sturdy and constructed of steel or aluminum. There are three parts to the cooker; the housing, the pot, and the lid that locks into place. You can most often find electric pressure cookers that are between three quarts and six quarts.

The Benefits of Using an Electric Pressure Cooker

The main benefit to cooking this way is that when you make your foods in an electric pressure cooker, they are retaining more of their nutrients than when you prepare them in other ways. Cooking times are shorter and there's less liquid involved.

The longer you cook food, the more you're cooking off valuable ingredients like vitamins, minerals, and proteins. Pressure cooking will not do that to your food. You'll reduce your cooking time by up to 70 percent, leaving all the flavor and the nutrients in what you eat. The temptation to simply order a pizza or throw something in the microwave instead of preparing a healthful meal will be eliminated. You always have time to throw something together in your cooker.

Another benefit is that the electric pressure cooker is environmentally sound. You're using less energy with this cooking tool than you would use with your oven or stovetop. The one-pot cooking technology will reduce your cleanup and your electric or gas bill. It also keeps your kitchen cooler.

Tips for Cooking in Electric Pressure Cooker

Keep it simple at the start

Let's be honest: it's going to take you a while to familiarize yourself with the variety of functions with which an electric pressure cooker is equipped. You need to keep things simple, especially if you are a first-time user. Rather than trying your hand at a complex cooking method, try something easy first, like boiling eggs or warming up a dish.

Familiarize yourself with pressure release methods

There are two ways to release pressure in an electric pressure cooker, the "quick pressure release" or the "natural pressure release." The "quick pressure release" happens when the valve is opened manually, and the steam is released quickly. As the steam is released, so is the pressure. When all of the pressure is released, the valve sinks and the lid is unlocked. For safety's sake, there is no way for the lid to open until the valve drops. Some steam will be given off, so watch your hands and don't stick your face too close just yet.

The "natural pressure release" happens when you let the pressure to decrease without opening the valve. After the allotted cooking time, the pressure cooker automatically switches from cooking mode to the "Keep Warm" mode. During this time, the pressure naturally drops. How long this takes depends on how much liquid is in the cooker. It can take anywhere from 10 minutes to half an hour. The valve will drop when it is time.

What specific release method should you use? For vegetables, it is best to use the "quick pressure release," since vegetables will get soggy if overcooked. The "natural pressure release" method is a great way to let meats, soups, and stews simmer.

Familiarize yourself with electric pressure cooker buttons

Some electric pressure cooker models have a timer that can delay the start time for up to 24 hours. Here are the standard buttons on most electric pressure cookers:

Sauté: this sautés and can be adjusted up to **frying** and down to **simmer.** This function is also used to reheat food and to thicken sauces.

Keep Warm/Cancel: this will cancel a prior function while keeping the food warm.

Soup: this prepares most standard soups for 40 minutes at high pressure. The time can be manually adjusted by using the "-" or "+" buttons.

Meat/Stew: this prepares meats for 35 minutes at high pressure. Cooking time can be adjusted manually.

Bean/Chili: this prepares beans for 30 minutes at high pressure. Cooking time can be adjusted manually.

Poultry: this cooks chicken for 15 minutes at high pressure. Cooking time can be adjusted manually.

Rice: this prepares rice; the cooking time cannot be adjusted manually.

Multi-grain: this cooks at high pressure for 40 minutes. Cooking time can be adjusted manually.

Porridge: this cooks oatmeal at high pressure for 20 minutes. Cooking time can be adjusted manually.

Steam: this is used to steam foods such as vegetables in a steamer basket. It cooks at high pressure for 10 minutes.

The best way to really enjoy your electric pressure cooker is by getting as educated as you can about what it is and how it works. Pay attention to all the settings and the functions, and try them out. Older models of pressure cookers were often unpredictable. That's not the case anymore with the modern cookers.

Clean it regularly

You want to clean your pressure cooker every time you use it, and it's important not to put it in the dishwasher. Some pressure cookers have the pot piece that is dishwasher-safe, but consult your manual before you do that. Wipe out the pot with a wet sponge or rag, and use a mild soap if you need to scrape off or remove food bits. Never use anything abrasive that will scratch the cooker. Warm soapy water does the trick, and then you need to dry it completely.

To get the most effective use from your pressure cooker, make sure you use recipes that are specifically designed for this type of cooking tool. Make sure you use enough liquid when you're cooking, and don't try to fry anything in it because oil can damage the system. Use the best food ingredients you can find, and make sure you're willing to try new things.

Electric Pressure Cooking Safety

When you use a cooker like this, you're inviting extreme temperatures into your kitchen. That's going to help you achieve great tasting food, but it can be dangerous if you're not using the cooker correctly. Always follow the instructions in the manual of your specific pressure cooker. Never cook anything without the lid locked securely into place, and don't try to open it while it's cooking. Most cookers come with security features that won't allow you to open the lid when it's unsafe.

Check your equipment before and after you use it, to make sure everything is functional. Never overfill your pressure cooker. If you try to stuff too much food in there or you add too much liquid, you could be putting yourself at risk.

As you are introducing electric pressure cooker recipes to your cooking routine, you will find that the tool is easy to use, and the results are impressive. Your food will be tasty, full of flavor and able to maximize nutrients and ingredients in ways that other cooking methods cannot. Try the 87 delicious electric pressure cooker recipes in this book and maybe experiment with some new foods. You'll find that whether you're feeding a whole family or setting the dinner table for one, you're going to get an easy, efficient, and clean way to cook.

Chapter 2: Electric Pressure Cooker Breakfast Recipes

When you're putting together electric pressure cooker breakfast recipes, you want to make sure you're preparing food that is healthy, easy to make and fast. Whether you're someone who likes a big, hot breakfast or you prefer to grab and go, there are a number of recipes that will suit your needs and preferences. The first recipe even involves chocolate...and there's nothing wrong with starting your day with chocolate.

Almonds and Oats

Yield: 4 servings
Ingredients:
1 cup steel cut oats
3½ cups coconut milk
1 tablespoon butter
¼ cup sliced almonds
¼ cup chocolate chips
¼ teaspoon salt
1 teaspoon cinnamon
1 teaspoon nutmeg

Directions:
1. Set your pressure cooker to "sauté" and melt the butter in the pot.

2. Add the oats and toast for 3 minutes, stirring occasionally. You want them to smell toasty and begin to brown.

3. Add the milk, salt, cinnamon, and nutmeg. Seal the lid, select a high pressure setting and set your timer for 10 minutes.

4. After 10 minutes, carefully remove the lid and give everything a stir. Let it sit for five more minutes so the oats can thicken.

5. Add chocolate and almonds to the top and serve.

Electric Pressure Cooker Apple Cranberry Oats

Yield: 4–5 servings
Ingredients:
2 cups oats
2 cups whole milk
1 cup almond milk
3 cups water
3 large apples, peeled and diced
1½ cups cranberries
¼ teaspoon salt
½ teaspoon cinnamon
1 tablespoon lemon juice
2 teaspoon vanilla extract
2 tablespoons butter
¼ cup maple syrup

Directions:
1. In a bowl, soak the maple syrup with some vanilla extract for about an hour.

2. Add the butter to the electric pressure cooker and set it to "sauté." Add the oats and fry for about a minute.

3. Add the water, whole milk, followed by almond milk, and give it a stir. Transfer the maple syrup mixture and stir again.

4. Sprinkle in the cinnamon powder and salt, and cover the lid of the pot. Cook on high pressure for 10 minutes.

5. Add the lemon juice and gently mix.

6. Garnish with diced apples and cranberries and serve.

Rice Pudding Parfait

Yield: 6 servings
Ingredients:
1 cup white rice
1½ cups water
2 cups milk, divided
½ cup sugar
2 eggs
½ teaspoon vanilla extract
1 cup raisins
¼ teaspoon salt
½ teaspoon cinnamon
½ cup blueberries

Directions:
1. Place the rice, water, and salt in the pressure cooker.
2. Cook on high pressure for 3 minutes. Let the natural pressure release, wait for 10 minutes, then open the pressure cooker.
3. Add one cup of the milk and the sugar and cinnamon. Stir everything together.
4. In a separate bowl, mix the eggs with the other cup of milk. Add the mixture to the pressure cooker.
5. Set the cooking function to "sauté" and stir while cooking for 3 minutes, until the mixture starts to boil.
6. Add the raisins and leave the mixture to cool and thicken for 5 minutes. Top with blueberries.

Home Fries with Cheese

Yield: 4 servings

Ingredients:

1 pound small red potatoes, cut into cubes

1 cup low sodium chicken broth

1 tablespoon butter

¼ teaspoon salt

½ cup shredded parmesan cheese

1 teaspoon dried oregano

1 teaspoon dried rosemary

1 teaspoon dried parsley

Directions:

1. Melt the butter in the pressure cooker on "sauté."

2. Add the potatoes and stir for about 5 minutes, until they are coated with butter.

3. Add the chicken broth and herbs. Close the lid and cook on high for 5 minutes.

4. Remove from heat and sprinkle the potatoes with salt and cheese.

Gluten Free and Vegan Buckwheat Porridge

Yield: 4 servings
Ingredients:
1 cup buckwheat groats
3 cups coconut milk
1 large ripe banana, sliced
1 teaspoon cinnamon powder
1 teaspoon vanilla extract
¼ cup honey
¼ cup raisins
1 cup grated coconut
Some chopped walnuts

Directions:
1. Rinse the buckwheat with water and drain. Add to the electric pressure cooker. Pour in the coconut milk, sprinkle with the cinnamon powder, and add in the vanilla extract. Mix well.

2. Simmer this mixture for about 2–3 minutes.

3. Throw in the grated coconut, raisins, ripened banana, and honey, and cover the lid of the Electric pressure cooker. Cook on high pressure for 10 minutes.

4. Release the pressure slowly and remove the porridge into a large bowl.

5. Garnish with some chopped walnuts and serve.

Hard Boiled Eggs

Yield: 3 servings
Ingredients:
6 eggs
1 cup ice
4 cups water

Directions:
1. Place a steamer basket in the pressure cooker pot. You can also use a rack if you don't have a basket.
2. Place the six fresh eggs in the basket and pour one cup of the water into the pressure cooker.
3. Close the lid and set the pressure cooker to high for 7 minutes.
4. When cooking time is complete, carefully open the lid and remove the steamer basket.
5. Drop the eggs into a bowl that's filled with the remaining 3 cups of water and the ice.
6. Allow them to cool for 5 minutes.

Breakfast Casserole

Yield: 4 servings

Ingredients:

6 eggs

1 tablespoon butter

1 tablespoon milk

½ cup water

1 cup chopped ham

6 small red potatoes, chopped

Directions:

1. Melt the butter in the pressure cooker on "sauté."

2. In a bowl, beat the eggs with the milk.

3. Add all the ingredients to the pressure cooker and seal the lid.

4. Cook on high pressure for 5 minutes.

Pumpkin Porridge

Yield: 4 servings
Ingredients:
1 cup steel cut oats
½ cup pumpkin puree
3 cups water
1 tablespoon butter
¼ teaspoon salt
1 teaspoon brown sugar
Dash of cinnamon (or nutmeg)

Directions:
1. Melt butter in the pressure cooker pot on "sauté" for 2 minutes.
2. Add the oats, pumpkin, water, salt, and sugar.
3. Close the lid securely and cook on high pressure for 10 minutes.
4. Wait another 10 minutes for the natural pressure to release.
5. Top the porridge with cinnamon or nutmeg and serve.

Baked Egg Cups

Yield: 4 servings
Ingredients:
4 ramekins
4 eggs
4 slices of ham
4 slices of cheese
4 sprigs of fresh rosemary
2 teaspoons olive oil
1 cup water

Directions:
1. Pour the water into the pressure cooker.
2. Lightly rub olive oil around the insides of each ramekin.
3. Break the eggs one at a time and add one egg to each of the ramekins, then the ham and then the cheese.
4. Place the ramekins into the steamer basket and lower into the pressure cooker.
5. Close and lock the lid and set the cooking pressure to low. Cook for four minutes.
6. Once the pressure has been released, remove the ramekins and sprinkle with fresh rosemary.

Black Beans and Burrito Bowl

Yield: 4–6 servings
Ingredients:
1 large tablespoon olive oil
1 pound chicken breast (boneless)
1 large red onion, finely chopped
1 large yellow bell pepper, chopped
1 cup black beans, soaked for at least 4 hours
1 cup water
1 teaspoon sea salt
1 teaspoon cayenne pepper
1 bay leaf
1 teaspoon garlic powder
Cumin powder to taste
2 small cups of lettuce

For the rice
1½ cups rice
1½ cups water
1 tablespoon lemon juice

Directions:
1. Rinse the rice with water. In a large bowl (heatproof), add the rice, water, and lemon juice. Set it aside.

2. Heat the olive oil in the electric pressure cooker and set it to "browning." Lay the chicken pieces in it and cook until brown on both sides. Set it aside on a plate.

3. Add the onion, black beans, salt, pepper, garlic powder, cumin powder, bay leaf, and water to the Electric pressure cooker and mix well.

4. Lay the browned chicken pieces on top of this mixture.

5. Set the rice bowl into a steamer basket. Cover the lid of the pot and cook for 8 minutes on high pressure.

6. Once the pressure has eased, make burritos by layering the bean mixture, rice, and lettuce leaves.

Eggs and Cheese Casserole

Yield: 6 servings
Ingredients:
6 large eggs
1 chopped small onion
1 cup diced ham
¼ cup heavy cream
1 cup diced cheddar cheese
1 teaspoon Herbs de Provence
Salt and pepper to taste

Directions:
1. In a bowl, beat the eggs and heavy cream until fluffy. Add the remaining ingredients to the bowl and stir.
2. Place the egg mixture in a heatproof bowl or dish; cover the dish.
3. Pour 1 cup water into the bottom of the electric pressure cooker. Place the heatproof dish inside the electric pressure cooker.
4. Close both the lid and the vent valve. Press the "Manual" button, and cook on high pressure for 20 minutes.

Hash Browns with Bacon

Yield: 6 servings
Ingredients:
2 pounds peeled russet potatoes
2 tablespoons olive oil
3 teaspoons chopped parsley
1 cup bacon, cooked and crumbled
Salt and pepper to taste

Directions:
1. Finely grate the potatoes. Dry them thoroughly with a paper towel. The drier the potatoes, the crispier they will be.
2. Pour the olive oil into the electric pressure cooker and set it to "Sauté."
3. Transfer the potatoes into the electric pressure cooker. Cook on medium heat for 5–6 minutes.
4. Stir in the bacon and parsley. Use a spatula to press down firmly on the potatoes.
5. Lock the lid on the electric pressure cooker. Hit "Low Pressure" and cook for another 6 minutes.
6. Open by using the "quick pressure release" method.
7. Serve with eggs.

Creamy Quinoa

Yield: 6 servings
Ingredients:
2 cups quinoa, rinsed
2½ cups water
2 tablespoons brown sugar
½ teaspoon vanilla extract
1/3 teaspoon cinnamon
Dash of salt

Directions:
1. Add all of the ingredients to the electric pressure cooker. Stir thoroughly to combine.

2. Cook for 1 minute on high pressure.

3. Let sit for 10 minutes.

4. Use the "quick pressure release" method to release any pressure.

5. Remove the lid carefully. Serve quinoa with milk, almond slivers, and berries.

Egg Croissants

Total Time: 18 minutes
Ingredients:
4 large eggs
Salt and pepper to taste
4 slices of cooked bacon, broken into small pieces
5 tablespoons shredded cheddar cheese
1 green diced scallion
4 croissants

Directions:
1. Place a steamer basket inside the electric pressure cooker and pour in 1½ cups water.
2. Whip the eggs in a bowl. Add the bacon pieces, cheese, and scallion to the eggs. Mix well.
3. Divide the mixture into 4 muffin cups. Transfer the filled muffin cups onto the steamer basket.
4. Shut the lid and cook on high pressure for 8 minutes.
5. When the beeper goes off, wait a few minutes and use the "quick pressure release" method.
6. Lift the muffin cups out of the electric pressure cooker.
7. Slice 4 croissants in half and stuff with the muffin cup content.

These electric pressure cooker breakfast recipes will be satisfying, easy to make and simple to clean up. You can include all different varieties, especially when it comes to the oatmeal and the porridge. Feel free to add different fruits and flavors. If you're a vegetarian, substitute the ham in these recipes for the breakfast veggie of your choice.

Chapter 3: Electric Pressure Cooker Chicken and Turkey Recipes

When you want to use your pressure cook to prepare high protein, low fat meals, consider building your plate around poultry. Chicken and turkey are tasty ways to eat healthy. These electric pressure cooker chicken and turkey recipes will give you the variety and the flavor you're looking for. Eating the same grilled piece of chicken meal after meal gets old fast. Liven things up a little with one of these choices.

Chicken Teriyaki

Yield: 4 servings
Ingredients:
1½ pounds boneless chicken breast
1 can pineapple
1 cup chicken stock
¼ cup brown sugar
½ cup soy sauce
¼ cup apple cider vinegar
1 tablespoon ground ginger
1 tablespoon garlic powder
1 teaspoon black pepper
1 tablespoon cornstarch
1 tablespoon water

Directions:
1. In a bowl, combine the brown sugar, soy sauce, vinegar, ginger, garlic powder and pepper until the sugar dissolves.

2. Place the chicken breasts in the pressure cooker and top with pineapple and chicken stock.

3. Pour the sugar mixture on top of that. Stir carefully to coat the chicken.

4. Set the pressure cooker to high pressure, and cook for 20 minutes.

5. Once the pressure is released, remove the chicken from the cooker but keep the liquid.

6. Add the cornstarch and water to the liquid and stir until it thickens. Use as a teriyaki sauce over the chicken.

Lemon Coconut Chicken

Yield: 6 servings
Ingredients:
1 cup coconut milk
¼ cup lemon juice
Some lemon zest
1 teaspoon turmeric powder
1 tablespoon curry powder
1 cup broccoli florets
4 pounds chicken thighs and breasts
1 teaspoon salt

Directions:
1. Roast the broccoli florets in a pan for 3–4 minutes.
2. In an electric pressure cooker, add the coconut milk, lemon juice, turmeric powder, curry powder, and salt and mix well.
3. Slide in the chicken pieces. Sprinkle in lemon juice and stir again. Cover the lid of the pot and cook for 15 minutes on high pressure.
4. When the time is up, gently release the pressure, remove the chicken, and place in a large bowl.
5. Sprinkle some lemon zest on top and add the broccoli florets. Serve hot.

Turkey Goulash

Yield: 4 servings

Ingredients:

2 pounds ground turkey breast

1 15-ounce can of diced tomatoes

2 cloves garlic, chopped

1 red onion, sliced

1 red bell pepper, chopped

1 green bell pepper, chopped

1 cup chicken stock

1 tablespoon butter

Directions:

1. Heat the butter in the pressure cooker and set it to "sauté." Add the ground turkey, cooking it for 5 minutes.

2. Add the tomatoes with their juices, the garlic, onion, peppers, and chicken stock. Cover and set on high pressure.

3. Cook for 15 minutes.

Whole Cooked Chicken

Yield: 6 servings

Ingredients:

1 4–5 pound roaster chicken
1 cup of water
1 cup chicken stock
4 cloves garlic, whole
3 carrots, chopped
2 celery stalks, chopped
1 onion, quartered
Salt and pepper

Directions:

1. Rinse the chicken, pat dry with paper towels and season generously with salt and pepper.

2. Place it in your pressure cooker on top of a cooking rack.

3. Add the vegetables and the water and chicken stock.

4. Cook for 25 minutes on high pressure.

Pina Colada Chicken

Yield: 4 servings
Ingredients:
2 pounds chicken thighs, cut into small pieces
1 cup diced pineapple
½ cup coconut cream
½ teaspoon salt
1 teaspoon ground cinnamon
¾ cup green onion, chopped
2 tablespoons desiccated coconut shavings
1 tablespoon arrowroot powder
1 tablespoon water

Directions:
1. Add all the above ingredients to an electric pressure cooker except for the green onions and mix well.

2. Set the "poultry" button and cook for 15 minutes on high pressure.

3. Release the steam.

4. Add the arrowroot powder to a tablespoon of water, mix, and add it to the chicken. Let it simmer for a few minutes until it thickens.

5. Garnish with chopped green onions and serve.

Chicken Taco Salad

Yield: 8 servings

Ingredients for Tacos:

15 ounces diced tomatoes

½ cup diced onion

3 minced garlic cloves

2 tablespoons tomato paste

Salt and pepper to taste

¼ teaspoon coriander

¼ teaspoon cocoa powder

1 teaspoon cumin

1 teaspoons chili powder

2 pounds boneless, skinless chicken meat

Ingredients for Salad:

10 cups torn romaine lettuce

1 can black beans

1 cup chopped cilantro

4 chopped scallions

1 corn kernels

2 cups cherry tomatoes, sliced in half

1 cup cubed or shredded cheddar, Pepper Jack, or Monterey Jack

½ cup chopped olives

1 diced avocado

tortilla chips and ranch dressing

Directions:

1. Stir all taco ingredients, except the chicken, into an Electric pressure cooker.

2. Place the chicken on top of the ingredients. Cook on high pressure for 8 minutes.

3. Allow pressure to release naturally.

4. Transfer the chicken to a platter and shred the meat.

5. Place the sauce in a blender and puree for smoothness.

6. Combine all salad ingredients in a bowl. Top with the chicken.

7. Drizzle the sauce over the salad.

8. Serve with ranch dressing and tortilla chips

Turkey Meatballs

Yield: 6 servings

Ingredients:

1½ pounds ground turkey breast

1 cup breadcrumbs

1 onion, diced

2 cloves garlic, minced

¼ cup milk

1 teaspoon dried Italian seasoning

1 egg

2 tablespoons ketchup

1 can whole tomatoes

1 cup water

Directions:

1. Make the meatballs by combining the turkey breast, breadcrumbs, onion, garlic, milk, seasoning, egg, and ketchup.

2. Use your hands to combine all those ingredients and form small balls.

3. Pour the whole tomatoes, with their juices, into the pressure cooker and add water. Mix the liquids together.

4. Add the meatballs. Cook on high pressure for 8 minutes.

5. Once the pressure is released, remove the meatballs and cover them with the sauce.

Barbecue Chicken

Yield: 4 servings

Ingredients:

2 chicken breasts, split in half

1 cup chicken stock

½ cup water

1 teaspoon nutmeg

1 teaspoon cinnamon

1 teaspoon ginger

1 teaspoon salt

1 teaspoon pepper

1 bottle barbecue sauce (use your favorite)

Directions:

1. Combine the salt, pepper, ginger, cinnamon, and nutmeg in a small bowl and rub the mixture into the chicken breasts.

2. Place them in the pressure cooker and cover with the water and the chicken stock.

3. Set the cooker on high pressure and cook for 15 minutes.

4. When the pressure releases, remove the chicken and cover with barbecue sauce.

Simple Herb Turkey Breast

Yield: 6 servings

Ingredients:

3 pounds turkey breast
1 can chicken broth (14 or 15 ounces)
1 red onion, quartered
3 stalks celery, roughly chopped
1 sprig fresh thyme
2 sprigs fresh rosemary
1 teaspoon dried basil
1 teaspoon dried oregano
Salt and pepper

Directions:

1. Season turkey breasts with salt, pepper, dried basil, and dried oregano.

2. Place a trivet at the bottom of the cooker and pour in the chicken broth.

3. Add the rosemary and thyme.

4. Place the turkey on top, breast side up. Add the onion and celery.

5. Cook on high pressure for 20 minutes.

Sweet Garlic Chicken

Yield: 6 servings

Ingredients:

3 pounds chicken drumsticks and thighs
2 cloves garlic, minced
2 teaspoons garlic Sriracha chili sauce
1 cup soy sauce
½ cup ketchup
1 cup honey
2 tablespoons brown sugar
2 tablespoons fresh basil, chopped
Salt and pepper
1 tablespoon cornstarch
1 tablespoon water

Directions:

1. In a bowl, whisk together the garlic, chili sauce, soy sauce, ketchup, honey, and brown sugar until the sugar dissolves.

2. Pour the mixture into the pressure cooker.

3. Season the chicken pieces with salt and pepper, and place them into the cooker.

4. Cook on high for about 10 minutes.

5. Allow the pressure to release, and take the chicken out of the pot.

6. Stir in the cornstarch and the water, allowing the sauce to thicken. Pour it on top of the chicken before you serve.

Cacciatore Chicken

Yield: 4 servings
Ingredients:
6 chicken thighs
1 large yellow onion, chopped
1 cup chicken broth
1 bay leaf
1 teaspoon garlic powder
1 teaspoon oregano
¾ cup black olives
1 teaspoon salt
6 medium tomatoes, chopped

Directions:
1. Heat the electric pressure cooker by setting it on "sauté" mode.

2. Slide the chicken thighs into the pot. Add chopped onion, bay leaf, chicken broth, garlic powder, oregano, salt, and tomatoes and mix well. Close the lid and cook this mixture for 15 minutes on high pressure.

3. When the pressure has been released, remove the mixture to a large plate.

4. Garnish with some olives and serve.

Honey Bourbon Chicken

Yield: 6 servings
Ingredients:
2 pounds cubed chicken thighs
2 tablespoons olive oil
2 diced garlic cloves
1 teaspoon minced ginger
½ teaspoon red pepper flakes
3 tablespoons ketchup
4 tablespoons brown sugar
¼ cup apple juice
1½ tablespoons apple cider vinegar
½ cup water
5 tablespoons soy sauce
¼ cup Bourbon (optional but delicious)
3 sliced green onions

Directions:
1. Use a bowl to mix the garlic, ginger, pepper flakes, vinegar, apple juice, ketchup, brown sugar, and soy sauce.

2. Place the chicken in the bowl and let marinate for half an hour.

3. Set the electric pressure cooker to "Sauté" and let heat up.

4. Add the olive oil and brown the chicken thighs. This can be done in batches.

5. Cover the chicken thighs with the marinade liquid.

6. Shut the lid and cook for 7 minutes on high pressure.

7. When the Electric pressure cooker beeps, wait 10 minutes for natural pressure release.

8. Open the lid, add the Bourbon if you are using, as well as the green onions, and select the "Sauté" option. Let simmer until the sauce thickens.

9. Serve with rice.

When you are thinking about these electric pressure cooker chicken and turkey recipes, remember that chicken and turkey can be used interchangeably. If you happen to have one in the fridge but not the other, you can use ground chicken instead of turkey or turkey breasts instead of chicken. Enjoy trying these fun foods that can come straight out of your pressure cooker and onto your plate in a matter of minutes.

Chapter 4: Electric Pressure Cooker Beef, Pork, and Lamb Recipes

A major part of any healthy and balanced eating program is protein. Beef and pork are packed with protein, and when you cook them in an electric pressure cooker, you get juicy, flavorful pieces of meat that taste delicious. These electric pressure cooker beef and pork recipes are sure to get your mouth watering. They are easy to prepare, mess-free and you'll be able to put them on the table in no time at all.

Best Barbeque Pork

Yield: 8 servings
Ingredients:
4 pounds pork roast
2 cups water
1 bottle of your favorite bbq sauce
1 teaspoon garlic powder
1 teaspoon salt
1 teaspoon pepper

Directions:
1. Rub the roast with the garlic powder, salt, and pepper. Place it inside the pressure cooker and cover with the water.

2. Close the lid, set the pressure and cook for 40 minutes.

3. Release the pressure and remove the pork roast from the cooker. Shred it and mix with the barbeque sauce.

4. Add a little of the liquid from the pressure cooker if you need to thin out the barbeque sauce at all.

Braised Beef Stew

Yield: 4 servings

Ingredients:

1 pound beef, cut into chunks

2 cloves garlic

2 tablespoons olive oil

2 potatoes

1 Vidalia onion

2 carrots

1 14/15 ounce can of green beans

2 15-ounce cans diced tomatoes

2 tablespoons flour

½ cup water

1 teaspoon salt

1 teaspoon pepper

1 teaspoon dried oregano

Directions:

1. Toss the beef chunks in the olive oil until coated, then cover with the flour.

2. Place the beef in the pressure cooker and stew the meat until it begins to brown.

3. Cut the potatoes, onion and carrots into bit sized pieces and add to the pressure cooker.

4. Add the garlic and then the cans of green beans and tomatoes, with their liquid.

5. Season with salt, pepper, and oregano.

6. Pour the water into the cooker and then set the pressure on high.

7. Lock the lid and cook for 15 minutes.

Maple Smoked Brisket

Yield: 4 servings
Ingredients:
1½ pounds beef brisket
2 tablespoons brown sugar
2 teaspoons sea salt
1 teaspoon ground pepper
1 teaspoon mustard powder
1 tablespoon onion powder
½ teaspoon garlic powder
½ teaspoon paprika powder
1 tablespoon olive oil
2 cups of chicken broth
1 tablespoon liquid smoke
Some fresh thyme leaves

Directions:
1. If the brisket is refrigerated, ensure you take it out and let it sit at room temperature for about 30 minutes.

2. In a bowl, combine brown sugar, sea salt, ground pepper, mustard powder, onion powder, garlic powder, and paprika powder.

3. Lay the brisket on a tray. Generously coat the meat with the above mixture.

4. Grease the bottom of the electric pressure cooker with olive oil. Heat for about 3 minutes on "sauté" setting.

5. Transfer the brisket to the pot and cook on both sides until golden brown. Make sure you don't burn the brisket while doing this.

6. Next, pour the chicken broth on top of the brisket, followed by liquid smoke. Close the lid, and let it cook for 50 minutes on high pressure.

7. Serve with some thyme leaves on top.

Swedish Meatballs

Yield: 8 servings

Ingredients:

1 pound ground beef

1 pound ground pork

6 tablespoons chopped parsley

2 teaspoons onion powder

1 teaspoon sage

¼ teaspoon allspice

Salt and pepper to taste

1 large diced onion

1½ cups sliced mushrooms

½ cup beef broth or coconut milk

Directions:

1. Use a bowl to combine the beef, pork, half the parsley, onion powder, sage, allspice, salt, and pepper. Form 1-inch meatballs.

2. Place the onion, mushrooms, and liquid into the electric pressure cooker.

3. Transfer the meatballs to the electric pressure cooker.

4. Lock the lid and activate the "Meat" function. Cook for 35 minutes.

5. Use the quick release method to release pressure. Transfer the meatballs to a platter with a slotted spoon.

6. Pour the sauce into a blender and puree it into a smooth gravy.

7. Spoon the gravy over the meatballs and garnish with remaining parsley.

8. Serve over noodles or rice.

Super Sausage and Peppers

Yield: 4 servings

Ingredients:

4 sweet Italian sausages

4 spicy Italian sausages

4 large bell peppers (any color)

1 15-ounce can diced tomatoes

1 15-ounce jar tomato sauce

1 cup water

1 red onion

4 cloves garlic, minced

2 tablespoons dried Italian seasoning

Directions:

1. Pour the tomatoes (with juices) and the tomato sauce into the pressure cooker.

2. Add the water, garlic, and Italian seasoning.

3. Chop the peppers and the onion into strips or chunks.

4. Add the sausages to the pressure cooker and top them with the peppers and onions.

5. Lock the lid into place and cook on high for 20 minutes.

Corned Beef and Cabbage

Yield: 4 servings
Ingredients:
3 pounds corned beef
4 cups beef broth
3 cups water
2 cloves garlic, minced
3 tablespoons spicy mustard
1 teaspoon whole peppercorns
1 head of cabbage, shredded
4 carrots, chopped
2 potatoes, cut into chunks

Directions:
1. Rinse the corned beef and place it in the pressure cooker on a rack, with the fat part of the meat facing up.

2. Cover with broth and water.

3. Add the garlic, mustard, and peppercorns.

4. Cover the pressure cooker and set the pressure to high. Cook for 45 minutes.

5. While it's cooking, place the cabbage, carrots, and potatoes into a basket.

6. When the corned beef is done, remove it carefully and place the basket of veggies into the same cooking liquid. Cook for three minutes.

Mongolian Beef

Yield: 6 servings
Ingredients:
2 pounds steak, sliced
1 tablespoon coconut oil
4 garlic cloves, minced
3 tablespoons dark soy sauce
½ cup water
3 tablespoons brown sugar
1 teaspoon minced ginger
2 tablespoons corn flour
3 medium-sized white onions, finely chopped
Salt and pepper to taste
Some chives

Directions:
1. Lay the steak on a tray. Season it with salt and pepper from all sides.

2. Grease the electric pressure cooker with coconut oil and set it to "browning." As the oil starts sizzling, transfer the steak in batches. Once browned on both sides, set it aside.

3. Add some coconut oil to the electric pressure cooker and set it to "sauté." Throw in the minced garlic, ginger, and chopped onions and sauté for 2-3 minutes. Add soy sauce and water and give it a stir.

4. Transfer the browned beef to the pot, set it on "high" and cook for 15 minutes.

5. Combine the cornstarch with water in a bowl and whisk. Pour this mixture into the pot, stirring continuously. Bring it to a boil until it thickens.

6. Serve with some chopped chives on top.

Pork Chops with Mushrooms

Yield: 4 servings

Ingredients:

4 thick pork chops

2 tablespoons olive oil

1 15-ounce can of tomato soup

1 bell pepper, chopped

1 red onion, chopped

6 carrots, chopped

6 small red potatoes

2 cups button mushrooms, chopped

Directions:

1. Rub the pork chops with olive oil and cook in the pressure cooker until they begin to brown.

2. Add peppers, onions, carrots, potatoes, and mushrooms.

3. Add the tomato soup. Secure the lid and cook on high pressure for about 15 minutes.

Pork Wraps

Yield: 4 servings
Ingredients:
2 pounds pork shoulder, chopped
1 tablespoon roasted and ground cumin
1 teaspoon ground pepper
1 teaspoon oregano
1 teaspoon ground cinnamon
3 garlic cloves, minced
1 dried chipotle pepper
1 cup tomatoes, diced
3 cups orange juice
1 teaspoon salt
Some lettuce, sliced cucumber pieces, sliced onion
4 tortillas

Directions:
1. Trim the fat from pork shoulder and add it to the electric pressure cooker. Add the rest of ingredients except the lettuce, cucumber, and onion, and mix well.

2. Cook this mixture for 20–22 minutes on high pressure.

3. When the pressure has released, take the mixture from the pot.

4. Fill the tortillas with this mixture, layering with lettuce leaves, cucumbers, and onion slices.

5. Serve on a large plate.

Sesame Beef & Broccoli

Yield: 4 servings

Ingredients:

1 pound beef roast

2 tablespoons sesame oil

1 onion, chopped

3 cloves garlic, minced

1 cup beef broth

½ cup soy sauce

1/3 cup brown sugar

½ teaspoon red pepper flakes

1 pound broccoli

¼ cup peanuts

2 tablespoons sesame seeds

Salt and pepper

Directions:

1. Coat the beef with sesame oil and season with salt and pepper, then place in the pressure cooker to brown.

2. Add onion and garlic and sauté for 2 minutes.

3. Add broth, brown sugar, soy sauce, red pepper flakes. Cook another two minutes.

4. Cover the pressure cook and set to high. Cook for 10 minutes.

5. Steam the broccoli while the beef cooks, in the microwave or stovetop.

6. Toss it all together.

Balsamic Pot Roast

Yield: 4 servings
Ingredients:
1 tablespoon sesame oil
3 lbs. chuck roast
1 tablespoon salt
1 tablespoon garlic powder
1 tablespoon onion powder
¼ cup balsamic vinegar
2 cups of water
1 medium onion, finely chopped
Some fresh parsley
Ground pepper to taste

Directions:
1. Lay the roast on a large plate. Season it with salt and pepper.
2. Heat the sesame oil in an electric pressure cooker on "sauté" and add the roast to it.
3. Fry the roast from both sides until thoroughly brown. Make sure not to burn it.
4. Pour some balsamic vinegar on top of the roast and cook it for about a minute.
5. Add onion and sauté for 2 minutes. Sprinkle some more salt, garlic powder, and onion powder and stir well.
6. Add the water, cover the lid, and cook for 35 minutes on high pressure.
7. When done, garnish with some fresh parsley and serve.

Pork Ribs

Yield: 4 servings

Ingredients:

2 pounds boneless pork ribs

1 tablespoon olive oil

3 tablespoons ketchup

1 teaspoon dried onion powder

1 teaspoon garlic salt

1 teaspoon pepper

1 teaspoon paprika

1 cup water

4 teaspoons white vinegar

1 tablespoon Worcestershire sauce

1 tablespoon Dijon mustard

Directions:

1. Coat the ribs in the oil and brown in the pressure cooker for about 5 minutes.

2. Sprinkle with onion powder, garlic salt, pepper and paprika.

3. Add water, ketchup, vinegar, Worcestershire sauce and mustard.

4. Cover and cook on medium-high for 15 minutes.

Pulled Pork Salad

Yield: 8 servings

Pork Ingredients:

2 pounds pork butt

1 cup chicken broth

3 chipotle peppers

1/3 cup diced chili peppers

¼ cup minced onions

3 diced garlic cloves

2 teaspoons olive oil

1 teaspoon cayenne pepper

½ teaspoon garlic powder

½ teaspoon cumin

Salt and pepper to taste

Salad Ingredients:

4 cups torn apart romaine lettuce

1 cup black beans

1 cup salsa fresca

½ cup plain yogurt

½ cup guacamole

Garnish with lime slices and cilantro

Directions:

1. In a bowl, mix the cayenne pepper, garlic powder, cumin, salt, and pepper together.

2. Rub the spice mix over the entire pork butt.

3. Set the electric pressure cooker on "Sauté." Add the olive oil and sauté the onion and garlic for 5 minutes.

4. Place the pork butt on top of the onion and garlic, and brown.

5. Transfer the pork butt to a platter.

6. Stir the broth, chili peppers and chipotles into the electric pressure cooker.

7. Transfer the pork butt back into the Pot. Lock the lid and set the "Meat" option on high. Cook for 50 minutes.

8. Transfer the pork butt to a platter and shred the meat. Stir the shredded meat back into the juices.

9. In a large bowl, mix the salad ingredients.

10. On serving plates, add the salad and top with shredded pork. Drizzle some of the juice over the salad.

Electric Pressure Cooker Lamb Shanks

Yield: 4 servings
Ingredients:
2 tablespoons ghee
3 pounds lamb shanks
1 teaspoon kosher salt
Ground pepper to taste
2 medium carrots, diced
2 celery stalks, chopped
1 large white onion, chopped
3 garlic cloves, minced
1 tablespoon thick tomato paste
1 pound fresh tomatoes, diced
1 cup chicken broth
1 teaspoon fish sauce
1 tablespoon apple cider vinegar
Some chopped parsley

Directions:
1. Grab the shanks, wash them properly, and season with salt and pepper. Set them aside.

2. Heat 1 tablespoon ghee in an electric pressure cooker on "sauté." Add the lamb shanks to it and brown on both sides. Place onto a tray.

3. Add the remaining ghee to the pot and throw in the chopped carrots, celery, onion, and minced garlic, and sauté for 4-5 minutes. Add the tomatoes and some tomato paste, and stir for about 2 minutes.

4. Transfer the browned lamb shanks to the electric pressure cooker, and add the chicken broth and fish sauce. Stir this mixture well.

5. Close the lid of the pot and cook for about 45 minutes on high pressure.

6. Serve with some chopped parsley on top.

These electric pressure cooker beef, pork, and lamb recipes are sure to give you a warm, hearty, and delicious meal any night of the week. Whether you're serving an entire family or cooking just for yourself and saving the leftovers, your pressure cooker takes hours off the time normally required to cook meat.

Chapter 5: Electric Pressure Cooker Seafood Recipes

Many people love seafood, and incorporating more fish into your diet is a great way to get protein and healthy fats without adding a lot of calories and saturated fats. Sometimes, cooking fish can seem boring; either you grill it, pan fry it or bake it with the requisite lemon and seasonings. The electric pressure cooker offers a new option. These electric pressure cooker seafood recipes will have you enjoying fish in a whole new way. Cooking it will be almost as enjoyable as eating it.

Ginger-Lemon Haddock

Yield: 4 servings
Ingredients:
4 filets of haddock
2 lemons
1-inch piece of fresh ginger, chopped
4 green onions
1 cup white wine
Salt and pepper to taste
2 tablespoons olive oil

Directions:
1. Massage the olive oil into the fish filets and sprinkle them with salt and pepper.
2. Juice your lemons and zest one of them.
3. Add that to the pressure cooker with the wine, onions, and ginger.
4. Place the fish in the steamer basket and lower it to the liquid.
5. Close the lid and cook on high for 8 minutes.

6. When the pressure is released, remove the fish and serve on rice or with a big salad.

Cod with Parsley and Piselli

Yield: 4 servings
Ingredients:
1 pound cod, cut into 4 filets
1 bag (10 ounces) frozen peas
1 cup fresh parsley
1 cup white wine
2 garlic cloves, smashed
1 teaspoon paprika
1 teaspoon oregano
1 sprig fresh rosemary

Directions:
1. In a small bowl, stir the wine and the herbs and spices together until blended.

2. Pour the liquid into the pressure cooker and add the frozen peas.

3. Place the fish into the steamer basket and close the lid. Cook on high heat for five minutes.

4. The peas will be mushy and soft, so plate those first and serve the fish on top.

Spicy Shrimp

Yield: 4 servings

Ingredients:

1 pound frozen shrimp, peeled and deveined
1 lemon, juiced
1 teaspoon black pepper
1 teaspoon white pepper
1 teaspoon cayenne pepper
1 can diced tomatoes (14–15 ounces)
1 jalapeno pepper, minced
2 cloves garlic, minced
1 sweet onion, minced

Directions:

1. Pour the tomatoes and juices into the pressure cooker.

2. Add the lemon juice, garlic and onion and stir.

3. Allow the frozen shrimp to rest at room temperature for 15 minutes. Then, add them to the pressure cooker.

4. Add the jalapeno and the black, white and cayenne peppers.

5. Mix everything. Cook on high pressure for 5 minutes.

Shrimp Fried Rice

Yield: 5 servings

Ingredients:

3 tablespoons sesame oil

2 large eggs

2 medium red onions, chopped

4 garlic cloves, minced

2 cups frozen shrimp, washed and tailed

1 cup peas

1 cup carrots

¼ cup soy sauce

2 cups brown rice

4 cups water

½ teaspoon cayenne pepper

1 tablespoon apple cider vinegar

½ teaspoon salt

1 teaspoon ginger, minced

Directions:

1. Set the electric pressure cooker on "sauté" and let it heat up for 2 minutes.

2. Add the sesame oil. Throw in the minced garlic and chopped onion and sauté until the onion turns slightly brown.

3. Next, slide in the chopped carrots and peas and fry for 4-5 minutes.

4. Add the shrimp, minced ginger, soy sauce, water, salt, pepper, and vinegar, and let simmer for 3-4 minutes.

5. Rinse the brown rice with water and add it to the pot.

6. Crack two eggs into the mixture and stir well. Cover the lid and set it to "rice" mode.

7. When the pressure has been released, transfer the rice to a large plate and serve.

Mediterranean Calamari

Yield: 6 servings

Ingredients:

2 pounds calamari or squid, chopped

2 tablespoons olive oil

1 red onion, sliced

3 cloves of garlic, chopped

1 cup red wine

3 stalks of celery, chopped

1 can (28 ounces) crushed tomatoes

3 sprigs fresh rosemary

½ cup Italian parsley, chopped

Salt and pepper

Directions:

1. Toss the calamari pieces in olive oil and salt and pepper.

2. To the pressure cooker, add the wine, tomatoes with their juices, celery, rosemary, garlic, and red onion.

3. Place the calamari in the steamer basket and lower it to the liquid. Cook on high for four minutes.

4. Remove the fish once the pressure has eased and sprinkle with fresh parsley.

Steamed Salmon

Yield: 4 servings
Ingredients:
4 salmon filets
2 cups water
4 Roma tomatoes
2 lemons
½ cup chopped shallots
4 sprigs fresh rosemary
Salt and pepper

Directions:
1. Slice the tomatoes and the lemons.
2. Make two foil pouches with two pieces of salmon each. Lay the salmon down on the foil and cover with salt and pepper, olive oil, a layer of tomatoes, a layer of lemons, a sprinkle of shallots and a sprig of rosemary. Fold up the foil so it creates a secure little package.
3. Pour the water into the pressure cooker and place the salmon into the steamer basket.
4. Cook on low heat for 15 minutes.
5. When the pressure has released, carefully unfold the packets.

Fish Chowder

Yield: 6 servings

Ingredients:

1 pound frozen tilapia filets

1 cup chicken broth

1 cup water

1 cup milk

1 cup heavy cream

6 red potatoes, chopped

1 cup frozen salad shrimp, peeled and deveined

3 stalks of celery, chopped

4 carrots, chopped

1 tablespoon dried thyme

1 tablespoon dried parsley

Directions:

1. Chop up the tilapia into small, bite-size pieces.

2. Add it to the pressure cooker with the salad shrimp, chicken broth, milk, water, potatoes, celery, and carrots.

3. Add the thyme and parsley and stir, until combined.

4. Cook in the pressure cooker on high pressure for 10 minutes.

5. Let the pressure release and lift the lid.

6. Stir in the heavy cream until everything in the pot thickens.

Seafood Paella

Yield: 6 servings

Ingredients for Fish Stock:

4–5 white fish heads

3 carrots

3 celery stalks

1 bay leaf

¼ cup unchopped parsley

6 cups of water

Ingredients for Paella:

4 tablespoons olive oil

1 diced onion

1 diced green pepper

1 diced red pepper

A few saffron threads

2 cups rice

2 cups fish stock

Salt and pepper to taste

2 cups chopped white fish and scallops.

2 cups mussels and shrimp

Directions for Fish Stock:

1. Place all of the ingredients inside the electric pressure cooker.

2. Set pressure to high and cook for 5 minutes

3. Use the natural pressure release option.

Directions for Paella:

1. Press the "Sauté" option on the electric pressure cooker. Heat the olive oil and sauté the peppers and onions for 4 minutes.

2. Add all the fish, rice and the saffron and continue sautéing for 2 minutes.

3. Stir in the fish stock, add the salt and pepper, and stir well.

4. Place the shellfish on top.

5. Shut the lid and cook on high pressure for 6 minutes.

6. Use the natural pressure release to release pressure.

7. Stir the paella and let sit for a few minutes.

Steamed Mussels

Yield: 3 servings

Ingredients:

3 pounds fresh mussels, cleaned and rinsed

1 can diced tomatoes (14 ounces)

1 cup white wine

1 tablespoon pepper

1 tablespoon dried parsley

Directions:

1. Pour the tomatoes into the pressure cooker with the juices and add the wine. Stir together and add the pepper and parsley.

2. Place the mussels in the steamer basket and cook on high pressure for 3 minutes.

3. Remove the lid when the pressure is released and cover the mussels with the tomato and wine sauce.

4. Serve with garlic bread.

Coconut Fish Curry

Yield: 5 servings

Ingredients:

1½ pounds fish steak (cut into small pieces)

1 tablespoon coconut oil

1 cup cherry tomatoes

2 small green chilies, slit open

2 medium onions, sliced

2 garlic cloves, minced

1 teaspoon coriander powder

2 teaspoons ground cumin

¼ teaspoon turmeric

Some curry leaves

1 teaspoon chili powder

3 tablespoons curry powder

2 cups coconut milk

¾ teaspoon salt

1 tablespoon lemon juice

1 teaspoon minced ginger

Directions:

1. Set the electric pressure cooker to "sauté" and heat the coconut oil.

2. Add curry leaves, minced ginger, garlic, and sliced onion and fry for 2-3 minutes.

3. Add some turmeric powder, ground cumin, and coriander powder and mix well.

4. Slide in the chilies and cherry tomatoes and sauté for another 2 minutes.

5. Pour in the coconut milk, add the salt and lemon juice, and bring to a boil.

6. Transfer the fish steaks and give the mixture a stir.

7. Cover the lid and cook for 5–7 minutes on high pressure.

8. Serve hot.

Seafood Gumbo

Yield: 10 servings
Ingredients:
1 cup flour
¾ cup canola oil
1 sliced onion
2 diced celery
1 cup diced green pepper
3 minced garlic cloves
3 tablespoons peanut oil
5 peeled and diced medium tomatoes
2 bay leaves
1 teaspoon cayenne pepper
½ teaspoon garlic powder
1 teaspoon paprika
1 teaspoon thyme
1 pound sliced Italian sausage
8 cups chicken stock
16 peeled raw shrimp without tails
20 cooked crawfish
3 cups lump crab meat
16 shucked oysters
Salt and pepper to taste

Directions:

1. Heat a skillet over medium heat, stir the flour and vegetable oil together for 3–4 minutes. (This is a roux.) Set aside.

2. Add the peanut oil to the electric pressure cooker and activate the "Sauté" function. Cook the peppers, onions, and garlic for 10 minutes.

3. Stir in the tomatoes, sausage, stock, and all of the spices.

4. Spoon in the roux while stirring.

5. Add all the seafood to the electric pressure cooker. Shut the lid and cook on high pressure for 8–10 minutes.

6. Release pressure naturally.

7. Serve Gumbo with rice.

Remember that most white fish is interchangeable. If you don't like cod or tilapia, use whatever fish you do enjoy. These electric pressure cooker seafood recipes are fast and easy to make, and they'll come from the cooker to your plate tasting fresh and healthy.

Chapter 6: Electric Pressure Cooker Soup Recipes

With these electric pressure cooker soup recipes, you'll never have to open a can of soup again. You'll be able to make fresh, delicious soups and stews within minutes. Whether you want a light lunch or a hearty meal served with crusty bread alongside a sandwich or a salad, these soups are bound to leave you feeling well-fed. They are easy and they're fun to try.

Chicken Noodle Soup

Yield: 6 servings
Ingredients:
2 chicken breasts
6 cups chicken stock
2 tablespoons olive oil
3 carrots, chopped
3 celery stalks, chopped
1 cup frozen peas
1 cup frozen corn
2 cups egg noodles
¼ cup fresh parsley
Salt and pepper

Directions:
1. Chop the chicken breast into small, bite sized pieces and toss with olive oil.

2. Put it in the electric pressure cooker to brown for about 5 minutes.

3. Add the carrots and celery as well as the salt and pepper. Let everything cook for 2 more minutes.

4. Add the chicken stock, the frozen peas and corn and the egg noodles. Stir everything together.

5. Seal the pressure cooker lid and cook on high for 8 minutes.

6. When the pressure reduces, sprinkle with parsley and serve.

Smoky Chicken Soup

Yield: 4 servings

Ingredients:

2 tablespoons olive oil, divided
1 medium onion, diced
2 garlic cloves, minced
4 cups chicken broth
3 chicken breasts
4 large tomatoes, diced
2 tablespoons thick tomato paste
¾ tablespoon chili powder
½ teaspoon smoked paprika powder
1 teaspoon sea salt
Ground pepper to taste
1 tablespoon lime juice
Some freshly chopped cilantro and sour cream for topping

Directions:

1. Set the electric pressure cooker to "sauté" and heat 1 tablespoon olive oil.

2. Add minced garlic and onion and sauté until the onion turns slightly golden brown.

3. Throw in the diced tomatoes and tomato paste and cook for about 3 minutes.

4. Add the chili powder, smoked paprika powder, sea salt, and ground pepper, and give it a mix.

5. Heat 1 tablespoon olive oil in another pan over medium heat. Place the chicken breasts in it and cook until slightly brown on both sides.

6. Transfer the chicken breasts to the Electric pressure cooker, followed by 4 cups of chicken broth. Add the lime juice and cover the pot with a lid. Cook for 10 minutes on high pressure.

7. Serve with some cilantro and sour cream on top.

Baked Potato Soup

Yield: 6 servings

Ingredients:

6 cups of potatoes, peeled and cubed

2 tablespoons butter

½ cup chopped shallots

4 cups of chicken broth

6 slices bacon, cooked and cooled

1 cup shredded cheddar cheese

1 cup shredded mozzarella cheese

2 tablespoons dried parsley

1 teaspoon cayenne pepper

2 tablespoons cornstarch

2 tablespoons water

2 cups heavy cream

Salt and pepper

Directions:

1. Melt the butter in the pressure cooker and add the shallots, stirring until coated.

2. Add 2 cups of the chicken broth, the parsley, cayenne pepper and salt and pepper. Stir.

3. Put the potatoes in a steamer basket and attach the lid. Cook on high for 5 minutes.

4. Release the pressure, and remove the potatoes.

5. Add the cheese to the mixture in the pressure cooker and stir until melted.

6. Add the remaining chicken broth and the heavy cream.

7. In a small bowl, mix the cornstarch and water together and add it to the pot.

8. Toss in the bacon and the cooked potatoes.

Creamy Tomato Soup

Yield: 4 servings

Ingredients:

6 large tomatoes

1 cup water

1 cup heavy cream

½ cup fresh basil leaves, chopped

1 tablespoon dried oregano

1 teaspoon salt

1 teaspoon white pepper

Directions:

1. Cut the tomatoes into halves and place them in the electric pressure cooker.

2. Add one cup of water. Cook on high for 5 minutes and allow pot to return to normal pressure.

3. Lift the lid and use an immersion blender to achieve a smooth consistency.

4. Add the cream, herbs and salt and pepper to taste.

Ham and Bean Soup

Yield: 4 servings
Ingredients:
1 pound dried black beans (or any favorite bean)
1 cup water
1 can (14/15 ounces) diced tomatoes
1 small onion, chopped
1 cup frozen peas
1 clove garlic
2 cups cubed cooked ham

Directions:
1. Put the dried beans in the electric pressure cooker and cover with water and tomatoes, in their juices.
2. Add the onion, peas, and garlic.
3. Cook on high pressure for 25 minutes and allow the pressure to ease.
4. Open the pot and stir in the cubed ham.

High Fiber Vegetable Soup

Yield: 6 servings
Ingredients:
1 tablespoon vegetable oil
4 garlic cloves, minced
1 cup carrots, chopped
1 cup green bell pepper, chopped
1 cup shredded cabbage
1 cup broccoli florets
½ cup kidney beans
¼ cup quinoa
1 teaspoon oregano
1 tablespoon soy sauce
1 teaspoon onion powder
4 cups of vegetable broth
¾ teaspoon salt
Some ground pepper
2 tablespoons lemon juice
Some basil leaves

Directions:
1. Set the electric pressure cooker to "sauté" and heat the vegetable oil.

2. Add minced garlic and sauté for about a minute.

3. Add remaining ingredients to the pot slowly, except for basil leaves and pepper. Stir well, using a large wooden spoon.

4. Close the lid and cook the soup for 5 minutes on medium pressure.

5. Let it release pressure and transfer to large soup bowls.

6. Season with some ground pepper and garnish with basil leaves.

Beef & Veggie Stew

Yield: 4 servings

Ingredients:

½ pound beef cut into small pieces

1 large potato, peeled and diced

2 tablespoons olive oil

1 cup water

½ red onion, diced

2 stalks celery, chopped

2 carrots, chopped

2 cups kale

1 can (14/15 ounces) diced tomatoes

4 cups beef broth

1 cup frozen green beans

1 cup frozen corn

1 teaspoon cumin

1 teaspoon paprika

Salt and pepper

Directions:

1. Toss the beef chunks in the olive oil and heat in the pressure cooker until they begin to brown.

2. Add the potato, onion, celery, carrots, kale, green beans, and corn.

3. Add the water, broth and the tomatoes with their juices.

4. Stir in the cumin and paprika.

5. Cook on high pressure for 30 minutes and sprinkle with salt and pepper to taste.

Beef Barley Soup

Yield: 6–8 servings
Ingredients:
8 cups beef stock
¾ cup pearl barley
1 pound sliced bella mushrooms
1 diced onion
2 diced carrots
2 diced celery stalks
3 minced garlic cloves
3 thyme sprigs
¼ teaspoon garlic powder
Salt and pepper to taste

Directions:
1. Combine all of the ingredients in an electric pressure cooker.
2. Cover the lid, and cook on high pressure for 20 minutes.
3. Allow the pressure to release for 10 minutes.
4. Use the "quick pressure release" method and serve hot.

Split Pea Soup

Yield: 4 servings
Ingredients:
1 cup dried split peas
2 cups chicken stock
4 slices Canadian bacon, chopped
1 onion, sliced
2 small red potatoes, chopped
2 cloves garlic, minced
½ cup cream
2 tablespoons fresh parsley
Salt and pepper

Directions:
1. Heat the bacon in the pressure cooker and as fat comes off the bacon, stir in the onion and garlic.

2. Add the chicken stock and the potatoes.

3. Stir in the cream and the peas until everything is combined.

4. Cook for 15 minutes on high pressure. Season with salt and pepper and parsley.

Butternut Squash Soup

Yield: 8 servings
Ingredients:
6 cups butternut squash, peeled and diced
1 large onion, chopped
3 large carrots, chopped
2 cups celery stalk, chopped
4 garlic cloves, minced
6 cups chicken broth
Some parsley leaves
1 teaspoon cayenne pepper
1 teaspoon salt
1½ cups coconut milk
2 teaspoon dried oregano
1 teaspoon paprika

Directions:
1. Add the butternut squash, chopped onion, carrots, minced garlic, celery, and salt to the electric pressure cooker.

2. Pour in the chicken broth, and bring this mixture to a boil. After that, set it on the "soup" function and cook until it reaches maximum pressure.

3. Once the time is up and the pressure has been released, open the lid and let the mixture cool down.

4. Using a hand blender, blend all ingredients into a fine paste. Add oregano, coconut milk, cayenne pepper, paprika powder, and salt and let it simmer for 10 minutes.

5. Garnish with some fresh parsley and serve.

Hot and Sour Soup

Yield: 4 servings

Ingredients:

½ pound chicken breast, cut into cubes

1 tablespoon sesame oil

3 cups chicken stock

2 tablespoons fresh ginger, grated

1 tablespoon freshly squeezed lime juice

1 whole chili pepper, sliced and seeded

1 tomato, chopped

½ cup fresh mushrooms, sliced

2 tablespoons fish sauce

2 tablespoons fresh cilantro

Directions:

1. Toss the chicken pieces in the sesame oil and heat in the electric pressure cooker for 5 minutes.

2. Add the chicken stock, ginger, lime juice, chili pepper, tomato, and mushrooms. Stir together.

3. Cook on high pressure for 10 minutes.

4. Once pressure is released, stir in the fish sauce and the cilantro.

Cauliflower Potato Soup

Yield: 6 servings

Ingredients:

6 slices of raw bacon, chopped

5 minced garlic cloves

1 medium diced onion

1 bunch chopped scallions

Salt and pepper to taste

1 chopped cauliflower

2 diced potatoes

4 cups chicken stock

¾ cup heavy cream

1 bay leaf

Directions:

1. Set the electric pressure cooker on "Sauté", add the bacon and cook for 4 minutes, until crisp.

2. Place bacon on a paper towel. Crumble after excess fat is absorbed.

3. Place the garlic, onion, and scallion in the Electric pressure cooker and cook for 1 minute. Season with salt and pepper.

4. Put some of the broth into the Electric pressure cooker and deglaze the bottom.

5. Add the cauliflower, potatoes, remaining broth, and bay leaf.

6. Shut the lid and cook on high pressure for 3 minutes.

7. Turn off heat and do a natural pressure release.

8. Open the lid. Remove the bay leaf.

9. Pour the soup into a large bowl and add the bacon bits and heavy cream.

10. Use an immersion blender to achieve a smooth consistency.

Lentil Soup

Yield: 6 servings
Ingredients:
2 cups lentils
3 minced garlic cloves
1 diced onion
1 tablespoon olive oil
2 teaspoons cumin
1 teaspoon paprika
2 sliced carrots
2 sliced celery stalks
1 pound Yukon potatoes
2 cups chopped spinach
6 cups water
Salt and pepper to taste

Directions:
1. Set the electric pressure cooker to "Sauté" and add the olive oil. Sauté the garlic, onions, cumin, paprika, celery, and potatoes for 5 minutes.
2. Add the lentils and stir.
3. Cover the ingredients with water.
4. Lock lid and cook for 3 minutes on high pressure.
5. Release pressure with the quick release option.
6. Mix in the spinach and adjust the seasoning.

Minestrone Soup

Yield: 6 servings
Ingredients:
2 tablespoons olive oil
2 stalks diced celery
1 large diced onion
3 cloves garlic, minced
1 diced carrot
1 teaspoon oregano
1 teaspoon basil
Salt and pepper to taste
28 ounces diced tomatoes
2 cups cannellini beans
4 cups vegetable broth
1 bay leaf
½ cup shredded spinach
1 cup elbow pasta
½ cup grated parmesan cheese

Directions:
1. Activate the "Sauté" setting of the electric pressure cooker.

2. Sauté the onion, carrot, celery, and garlic in the olive oil for 10 minutes. Top with salt, pepper, oregano, basil, diced tomatoes, bay leaf, broth, and pasta.

3. Shut lid and cook on high pressure for 6 minutes.

4. After the timer beeps, let soup sit for a few minutes. Use the quick release option.

5. Open the lid and add the white beans and the spinach. Stir well.

6. Garnish with the parmesan cheese and serve.

Oxtail Soup

Yield: 6 servings
Ingredients:
2 pounds oxtail, chopped into bite-sized pieces
2 diced tomatoes
2 diced celery stalks
2 diced carrots
1 sliced scallion
1 tablespoon vegetable oil
2 tablespoons tomato paste
Salt and pepper to taste
3 ginger slices, finely minced
½ cup white wine
5 cups water

Directions:
1. Place all of the ingredients in an electric pressure cooker.
2. Cook on high pressure for 45 minutes.
3. Let the pressure release naturally and allow steam to escape.
4. Serve hot.

These electric pressure cooker soup recipes will give you something hot and homey to enjoy in a matter of minutes. Even if you're cooking for one, you can make a big pot of soup and freeze the leftovers for later.

Chapter 7: Electric Pressure Cooker Dessert and Snack Recipes

Every good meal ends with a dessert, and whether you like yours simple or decadent, it's possible to create an impressive final course with your electric pressure cooker. Your mouth will water when you start gathering the ingredients for these electric pressure cooker dessert and snack recipes. With everything from chocolate to wine to cream - you're bound to find a favorite and make it a weekly treat.

Wine-Soaked Pears

Yield: 6 servings
Ingredients:
1 cup red wine
6 Anjou pears
1 vanilla bean
1 teaspoon cinnamon
2 whole cloves
¼ cup brown sugar

Directions:
1. Place the wine, vanilla, cinnamon, cloves, and sugar in the electric pressure cooker. Stir to combine everything.
2. Peel the skin off the pears, but leave the stems on.
3. Place them in the wine mixture, so that they are standing.
4. Cook on low pressure for 7 minutes.

Chocolate Cake with Jam

Yield: 8 servings
Ingredients:
1½ cups flour
4 tablespoons cocoa powder
¼ cup blackberry jam
1 cup milk
1 tablespoon salted butter, melted
¾ cup sugar
2 eggs
1 teaspoon baking powder
2 tablespoons confectioner's sugar

Directions:
1. In a bowl, sift together flour, cocoa powder, and baking powder.

2. In a separate bowl, whisk the eggs with the sugar and the melted butter. Stir in the jam until the ingredients are combined.

3. Slowly combine the flour mixture with the wet mixture. Add milk. Pour into a greased pan and place it into the pressure cooker on a trivet.

4. Cook on low pressure for 30 minutes.

5. Sprinkle with confectioner's sugar once the cake has cooled.

Nutty Fudge Pieces

Yield: 2 dozen fudge pieces

Ingredients:

1 12-ounce package of semi sweet chocolate chips

1 14-ounce can of condensed milk

½ cup walnuts

½ cup almonds

1 teaspoon vanilla

2 cups water

Directions:

1. Combine the milk and chocolate chips in a small or medium bowl (make sure it will fit in your pressure cooker).

2. Cover the bowl with aluminum foil.

3. Pour the water into the pressure cooker and set the rack so you can place the bowl on top of it in the cooker.

4. Cook on high pressure for 5 minutes.

5. Remove the bowl once the pressure has abated and take the foil off the bowl.

6. Stir in the nuts and vanilla until everything is combined.

7. Drop in unformed balls onto wax paper and allow to cool.

Sweet Rice Pudding

Yield: 6 servings

Ingredients:

1 cup uncooked long grain rice

¼ cup heavy cream

¼ cup sugar

1 cup water

2 cups milk

1 teaspoon vanilla

1 teaspoon cinnamon

1 teaspoon nutmeg

1 egg

½ teaspoon salt

1 tablespoon butter

Directions:

1. Melt the butter in the electric pressure cooker and add the rice, stirring to coat.

2. Add water, salt, milk, and sugar.

3. Press the lid into place and cook on high pressure for 7 minutes.

4. While it's cooking, mix the egg, cream, and vanilla in a separate bowl. Add a little bit of the hot cooking liquid from the pressure cooker to the egg mixture to temper it.

5. After you do this successfully, add the egg mixture to the pressure cooker.

6. Cook uncovered for about 5 minutes, until it begins to bubble.

7. Stir while it cools and sprinkle cinnamon and nutmeg on top.

Coconut Rice Pudding

Yield: 10 servings
Ingredients:
1 cup uncooked white rice
1½ cups water
2 teaspoons coconut oil
Dash of salt
14 ounces coconut milk (not coconut cream)
½ cup white sugar
2 large eggs
½ cup milk
1 teaspoon vanilla
Optional: Toasted shredded coconut

Directions:
1. Combine the rice, water, and coconut oil in the electric pressure cooker.
2. Cook for 5 minutes on high pressure.
3. Use the natural pressure release.
4. Stir in the coconut milk, vanilla, and sugar.
5. In a bowl, whip together eggs and milk. Pour the egg mixture in the Electric pressure cooker while stirring.
6. Press the "Sauté" option and stir until the mixture thickens.
7. Pour the rice pudding into individual dishes.
8. Serve warm. You can top with whipped cream and toasted coconut.

Green Tea Coconut Crème Brûlée

Yield: 4 servings
Ingredients:
1 tablespoon green tea powder
1½ cups whole cream
1 cup coconut milk (whole fat)
1½ teaspoons vanilla extract
¼ teaspoon salt
6 large egg yolks
8 tablespoons brown sugar, divided
Boiling water

Directions:
1. In a large bowl, combine coconut milk, cream, vanilla extract, salt, and mix well.

2. Heat this mixture in a small saucepan while continuously stirring.

3. In another bowl, whisk the egg yolks along with the brown sugar until all ingredients are blended.

4. Pour the cream mixture into the bowl and stir well.

5. Transfer the mixture to small ramekins or heatproof bowls. Be sure to fill only ¾ of the bowl with the mixture, so it leaves room for rising.

6. Add some boiling water to the electric pressure cooker and set on a trivet. Place the ramekins on it and close the lid. Cook for 5 minutes on high pressure and wait for the pressure to release on its own.

7. Refrigerate the ramekins for at least 4 hours.

8. Remove the ramekins and sprinkle some sugar on top. With the help of a blowtorch, melt the sugar until it turns brown, and serve.

Chocolate Mousse with Raspberries

Yield: 8 servings

Ingredients:
1 cup heavy cream
1 cup whole milk
¼ cup super-fine sugar
12 ounces dark cooking chocolate
6 egg yolks
1 teaspoon vanilla extract
1 tablespoon cocoa powder
6 fresh raspberries
2 cups of water

Directions:
1. Stir the cream, milk, and sugar in a saucepan on low heat until sugar dissolves. Add the chocolate pieces.
2. Whisk the egg yolks until they become thick and slowly add to the chocolate. Add the vanilla.
3. Pour the chocolate mixture into a greased ovenproof dish. Cover with foil.
4. Add the water to the electric pressure cooker and place the dish on a trivet.
5. Close the lid and cook for 20 minutes on high pressure.
6. Once it has cooled, remove the dish. Dust with cocoa powder and place the raspberries in the mousse.

Hot Chocolate Fondue

Yield: 4 servings
Ingredients:
One 100 g bar of dark chocolate
½ cup heavy cream
1 tablespoon sugar
1 teaspoon amaretto liquor

Directions:
1. Add some water into the electric pressure cooker and set a trivet inside.

2. In a bowl, add the chocolate, cream, sugar, and liquor and mix well.

3. Transfer the mixture into small ramekins and set them on the trivet.

4. Cover the lid of the pot and cook for 2 minutes on high pressure, then lower the heat and cook again for a minute.

5. Open the pot slowly and take out the ramekins. Using a spoon, stir the mixture in the ramekins for about a minute, so lumps aren't formed.

6. Serve with fresh fruit on the side.

Chocolate Brownies

Yield: 10–12 servings
Ingredients:
6 tablespoons unsalted butter
4 tablespoons unsweetened cocoa powder
1 cup sugar
¾ cup all-purpose flour
¼ teaspoon salt
¾ tablespoon baking powder
2 large eggs
¼ cup chopped walnuts
2 cups water

Directions:
1. In a small pan, melt the butter on the stove. Set aside and mix in the cocoa powder.

2. Mix the sugar, flour, salt, and baking powder in a small bowl. Add the eggs and walnuts and stir in the cocoa mix.

3. Transfer the batter to an 8" pan that's been greased. Use aluminum foil to cover.

4. Place the pan at the bottom of the electric pressure cooker.

5. Pour in the 2 cups of water.

6. Shut the lid and cook for 35 minutes on high pressure.

7. Use the natural pressure release option.

8. Let brownies cool and cut into 2" squares.

Molten Chocolate Mini Lava Cakes

Yield: 3 servings
Ingredients:
1 large egg
2 tablespoons olive oil
4 tablespoons all-purpose flour
4 tablespoons milk
4 tablespoons sugar
1 tablespoon cocoa powder
½ teaspoon baking powder
⅛ teaspoon salt
Optional but recommended: ½ teaspoon orange zest

Directions:
1. Grease 3 ramekins with butter.
2. Add 1 cup of water to the electric pressure cooker and insert a trivet.
3. Use a bowl to mix together all ingredients. Blend well.
4. Pour the batter into the ramekins. Leaving a bit of space at the top.
5. Transfer the ramekins to the Electric pressure cooker.
6. Shut the lid and cook for 6 minutes on high pressure for a soft inner cake.

Apples A La Mode

Yield: 4 servings
Ingredients:
4 red delicious apples
1 lemon
2 cups grape juice
¼ cup strawberry jelly
1 teaspoon pepper
½ vanilla bean
¼ cup crushed walnuts
4 cups ice cream

Directions:
1. Pour the juice and jelly into the electric pressure cooker. Set the cooker to "sauté," and heat while stirring until the jelly breaks down.

2. Grate the rind off the lemon and then cut the lemon in half and squeeze the juice into the pressure cooker. Add the rind.

3. Core the apples from the bottom, so the form stays intact. Coat the apples in the jelly mixture and then wrap them in aluminum foil.

4. Place the apples in a steamer basket.

5. Add the pepper and vanilla to the cooker and lower the apples. Cook for 10 minutes on high pressure.

6. Once cool and pressure is released, unwrap the apples and cover them with ice cream and walnuts.

Chunky Applesauce

Yield: 4 servings

Ingredients:

10 apples, cored, peeled and cut into chunks

¼ cup apple juice

¼ cup water

¼ cup sugar

2 teaspoons ground cinnamon

Directions:

1. Place the apples, liquid, sugar, and cinnamon in your pressure cooker.

2. Close the lid and cook for 5 minutes on high pressure.

3. When pressure releases, stir until apples break down to the level of consistency you prefer.

Tapioca Pudding

Yield: 4–6 servings
Ingredients:
½ cup tapioca pearls, soaked for at least 1 hour
1 cup whole milk
1 cup coconut milk
¾ cup palm sugar
Some lemon zest
Some chopped cashews for the pudding
5–6 roasted cashews for garnishing

Directions:
1. Add the soaked tapioca pearls, whole milk, coconut milk, palm sugar, chopped cashews, and lemon zest to an electric pressure cooker.
2. Set the pot to "sauté" and keep stirring the mixture until the sugar is completely dissolved.
3. Cover the lid of the pot and cook for 10 minutes on high pressure.
4. Let the pot stand for about 15 minutes.
5. Once the pressure has been released, open the lid.
6. Serve chilled with some roasted cashews on top.

Wine Poached Figs on Yogurt Crème

Yield: 2 servings
Ingredients:
4 large sized figs
1 cup red wine
¼ cup palm sugar or honey
½ cup assorted nuts (chopped cashews, almonds, and pistachios)
4 cups plain yogurt

Directions:
1. Pour the yogurt into a mesh strainer and place it in the fridge to drain for about 6 hours. Do not wait for too long or the yogurt might get too crumbly.

2. Wash the figs and pat them dry. Place them in the electric pressure cooker. Add the wine and sugar and cover the lid of the pot.

3. Cook on medium pressure for 6-7 minutes.

4. On serving plates, add the yogurt crème, and poached figs. Garnish with wine syrup and chopped nuts on top.

Creamy Artichoke Dip

Yield: 4 servings
Ingredients:
½ cup cannellini beans, soaked for about 4 hours
1 cup vegetable broth
8 medium sized artichokes
2 garlic cloves, minced
Half a lemon
¾ cup plain yogurt
¾ teaspoon salt
¼ teaspoon ground pepper
1 small cup grated ricotta cheese
Some nachos

Directions:
1. Wash the artichokes under running water and slice into halves.

2. Boil artichokes in water for 30 minutes. Remove the leaves and carefully remove the chokes using a spoon.

3. Add the artichokes to an electric pressure cooker. Add the minced garlic cloves, lemon, vegetable broth, and beans and mix well.

4. Cook this mixture for 20 minutes on high pressure.

5. Once the pressure has been released, open the lid.

6. Let the mixture stand for a few minutes. Now add yogurt, ground pepper, salt, and cheese and mix well.

7. Add these ingredients to a blender and combine until it forms a smooth paste.

8. Serve along with some nachos.

Candied Lemon Peels

Yield: about 80 strips
Ingredients:
1 pound lemons
3 cups brown sugar, divided
4 cups of water

Directions:
1. Wash the lemons thoroughly and pat them dry with paper towel.

2. Slice the lemons in half. Scoop out the pulp using a sharp knife.

3. Cut the lemon peel into thin strip. Add the peels to the electric pressure cooker, followed by 3 cups of brown sugar and the water.

4. Cover the lid and cook for 10 minutes on high pressure.

5. After the pressure has been released, drain the peels, lay them on a sheet, sprinkle some sugar on top and refrigerate overnight. Store in an airtight container for up to 6 weeks.

Crème Brule

Yield: 6 servings
Ingredients:
8 egg yolks
2 cups heavy cream
1/3 cup white sugar
¼ teaspoon salt
2 teaspoons vanilla
5 tablespoons powdered sugar

Directions:
1. Add 1 cup of water to the electric pressure cooker and insert the trivet.

2. In a bowl, beat the yolks and cream together. Add the remaining ingredients and stir well.

3. Fill 6 ramekins with the mixture. Cover with aluminum foil and transfer the ramekins on top of trivet.

4. Shut the lid and cook for 6 minutes on high pressure.

5. At the beep, use the natural pressure release for 10 minutes to release pressure.

6. Open the lid and transfer the ramekins to a rack. Uncover and let cool.

7. Cover the ramekins with plastic wrap and place in refrigerator for 2 hours.

8. Before serving, dust with the powdered sugar and light each Brule with a torch.

Tangy Sweet Potato Wedges

Yield: 4 servings
Ingredients:
3 large sweet potatoes
¾ teaspoon salt
1 tablespoon dry mango powder
1 teaspoon paprika
2 tablespoons vegetable oil
1 cup water

Directions:
1. Wash the sweet potatoes thoroughly and peel them. Cut into medium-sized wedges.

2. Add 1 cup water and place a trivet in the electric pressure cooker.

3. Lay the sweet potato wedges on it and cook for 15 minutes on high pressure.

4. When done, remove and place the wedges on a plate.

5. Heat the vegetable oil in a saucepan over medium-high heat. Slide in the sweet potato wedges and pan sear until they turn brown.

6. Combine dry mango powder, salt, and paprika in a bowl and mix well.

7. Coat the wedges generously with this mixture and serve.

Cheesecake

Yield: 6 servings
Ingredients for Cake:
16 ounces cream cheese at room temperature
½ cup white sugar
2 large eggs at room temperature
1/3 cup sour cream

Ingredients for Crust:
12 crumbled graham crackers
5 tablespoons melted butter

Directions:
1. Thoroughly mix the cracker crumbs with the melted butter.
2. Use fingers to push the crust into a 7" springform pan.
3. Place the springform pan in the freezer.
4. In a mixer, blend the cream cheese, sugar, eggs, and sour cream. Mix ingredients until smooth.
6. Retrieve the springform pan from the freezer and fill it with the cheesecake filling.
7. Pour a cup of water into the electric pressure cooker and insert in a trivet.
8. Place the cheesecake into the electric pressure cooker.
9. Shut the lid and cook for 25 minutes on high pressure.
10. Use the quick pressure release option.
11. Remove the springform pan when cooled.

Oreo Cheesecake

Yield: 6 servings

Ingredients for Crust:

¼ cup melted butter

12 crushed and crumbled Oreo cookies

Ingredients for Oreo Cheesecake:

16 ounces cream cheese, room temperature

½ cup granulated sugar

2 large eggs, room temperature

1 tablespoon all-purpose flour

¼ cup heavy cream

2 teaspoons vanilla

8 whole Oreo cookies, coarsely chopped

Directions:

1. Cover the bottom and sides of a 7" springform pan with aluminum foil. Butter the inside of the pan.

2. In a bowl, mix the crumbled Oreo cookies with the melted butter.

3. Use your fingers to press the crumb mix to the bottom of the springform pan. Place pan with crust in freezer for 15 minutes.

4. Use a mixer with a paddle attachment to whip the cream cheese until it is smooth. Combine with the sugar.

5. Add the eggs (must be at room temperature) and blend thoroughly.

6. Mix in the flour, cream, and vanilla and beat until the batter is smooth and creamy.

7. Stir in the chopped cookies.

8. Transfer the batter to the springform pan and cover with aluminum foil.

9. Insert a trivet into the electric pressure cooker and add 1½ cups of water.

10. Create a foil sling and place it on the trivet.

11. Set the springform pan on top of the foil and place the ends of the strips on top.

12. Cook on high pressure for 40 minutes.

13. At the beep, select "Keep Warm." Wait for 10 minutes and use the quick pressure release method.

14. Use the foil to lift the cake. Let cool.

15. Refrigerate the cheesecake for at least 8 hours.

Chocolate Apple Bundt Cake

Yield: 6 servings
Ingredients:
2 cups white sugar
3 large eggs
1 cup butter
½ cup water
1 teaspoon vanilla
2½ cups flour
3 tablespoons cocoa powder
1 teaspoon baking soda
1 teaspoon allspice
½ teaspoon cinnamon
2 cups grated apples
1 cup chocolate chips
1 cup chopped walnuts or pecans
½ cup raisins

Directions:
1. Grease the inside of a Bundt pan.

2. In a bowl, whip together the sugar, eggs, water, butter, and vanilla.

3. In another bowl, mix flour, cocoa powder, baking soda, cinnamon, and allspice.

4. Add the dry mixture to egg mixture. Add the chocolate chips, apples, nuts, and raisins.

5. Place half of the batter into the prepared Bundt pan. Use aluminum foil to cover the pan.

6. Pour a cup of water into the electric pressure cooker and insert a trivet.

7. Use a foil sling to place the pan in the Electric pressure cooker.

8. Cook for 35 minutes on high pressure.

9. Release pressure by the natural pressure release method for 10 minutes.

10. Let the cake cool on a rack or plate.

Note: This recipe has enough batter for 2 cakes.

There is no need to rely on an oven or the stovetop: These electric pressure cooker dessert and snack recipes are simple, delicious, and fast.

Conclusion

Cooking with an electric pressure cooker is a great way to prepare hot food, even when you're in a hurry. There's no longer any need to rely on fast but unhealthy foods. Enjoy incorporating these easy, delicious, and healthy electric pressure cooker recipes into your everyday eating.

Finally, I want to thank you for reading my book. If you enjoyed the book, please take the time to share your thoughts and post a review on the book retailer's website. It would be greatly appreciated!

Best wishes,

Amanda Hopkins